Instant Edublogs

Set up your blog, develop a thriving community
of readers, and reach out to your students

Jason T. Bedell

BIRMINGHAM - MUMBAI

Instant Edublogs

First published: September 2013

Production Reference: 1230913

Published by Packt Publishing Ltd.
Livery Place
35 Livery Street
Birmingham B3 2PB, UK.

ISBN 978-1-84969-862-7

www.packtpub.com

Credits

Author
Jason T. Bedell

Reviewer
Charlene V. Martoni

Acquisition Editor
Joanne Fitzpatrick

Commissioning Editor
Govindan K.

Technical Editors
Adrian Raposo
Dennis John

Project Coordinator
Sageer Parkar

Proofreader
Lawrence A. Herman

Production Coordinator
Conidon Miranda

Cover Work
Conidon Miranda

About the Author

Jason T. Bedell is currently working as a Technology Coordinator of a school. He has had the privilege of teaching students aged 4 to 18, and has been able to blog about the process for years. In addition, he is a web designer and programmer. He is constantly on the lookout for cutting edge technologies and tries to figure out how to use them to best serve his students.

He also runs JTB Consulting, a website and application development firm, which can be found at `jasontbedell.com`. In addition, he provides educational consulting and regularly speaks at schools and conferences.

> I'd like to thank my wife for providing the time and support to complete this book.

About the Reviewer

Charlene V. Martoni is a journalist and educator based out of the Hudson Valley in New York. She attended the State University of New York at New Paltz and she graduated with a dual bachelor's degree in Adolescence Education (English) and Journalism. She also graduated with a minor in the Visual Arts. Martoni has written for various publications in New York State, including *The Watershed Post*, *The Journal News*, and *The New Paltz Times*. She aspires to pursue a Master's degree in the Library and Information Sciences and advance towards her New York State Professional Teacher certification. To view Martoni's EduBlog, visit `MissMartoni.com`. You can also view her journalism portfolio at `CVMartoni.com`. She encourages other educators and writers to contact her via Twitter (`@CVMartoni`) or e-mail (`CVMartoni@gmail.com`).

I would like to thank my mentors from the State University of New York at New Paltz for their continuous support of my passion for journalism and education: Lisa Phillips, Adam Bosch, Howie Good, Jacqueline Denu, Lisa Barker, Julie Gorlewski, and Joe Dolan.

www.PacktPub.com

Support files, eBooks, discount offers and more

You might want to visit www.PacktPub.com for support files and downloads related to your book.

Did you know that Packt offers eBook versions of every book published, with PDF and ePub files available? You can upgrade to the eBook version at www.PacktPub.com and as a print book customer, you are entitled to a discount on the eBook copy. Get in touch with us at service@packtpub.com for more details.

At www.PacktPub.com, you can also read a collection of free technical articles, sign up for a range of free newsletters and receive exclusive discounts and offers on Packt books and eBooks.

http://PacktLib.PacktPub.com

Do you need instant solutions to your IT questions? PacktLib is Packt's online digital book library. Here, you can access, read and search across Packt's entire library of books.

Why Subscribe?

- ▸ Fully searchable across every book published by Packt
- ▸ Copy and paste, print and bookmark content
- ▸ On demand and accessible via web browser

Free Access for Packt account holders

If you have an account with Packt at www.PacktPub.com, you can use this to access PacktLib today and view nine entirely free books. Simply use your login credentials for immediate access.

Table of Contents

Preface

There are a lot of platforms that can help you start a blog or share your thoughts online. However, few are designed with the specific needs of educators in mind. Edublogs.org is designed with many special features to help educators to be more effective and reflective practitioners. It is powerful enough for advanced users, yet simple enough that newcomers will be able to get started easily without becoming distracted from teaching. This book will help you get up to speed quickly, from creating a blog to customizing and growing an audience.

What this book covers

Introducing Edublogs.org (Must know) will describe how to get started with the Edublogs blogging platform.

Choosing a style (Must know) will demonstrate how to choose a theme for the blog.

Navigating your dashboard (Must know) will introduce the Edublogs dashboard and how to use it to manage a blog.

Finding your niche (Must know) will illustrate how to find one's place in the blogging community.

Committing to a writing schedule (Should know) will describe how to provide a steady and predictable stream of content to readers.

Managing content (Must know) provides details about managing different types of content.

Growing an audience organically (Should know) details strategies for investing in and growing your readership.

Extending your reach with social media (Should know) will show some methods for growing an audience using social media.

Using plugins for greater engagement (Become an expert) will detail some of the advanced plugins that can be utilized with Edublogs Pro accounts.

Blogging with students (Become an expert) will look at different scenarios for blogging with students and how to set those up with Edublogs.

Analyzing statistics (Become an expert) will show how to utilize statistics to serve one's readers better.

What you need for this book

This book requires a working Internet connection and a browser.

Who this book is for

This book is for educators who are looking to start blogging or write publicly online.

Reader feedback

Feedback from our readers is always welcome. Let us know what you think about this book—what you liked or may have disliked. Reader feedback is important for us to develop titles that you really get the most out of.

To send us general feedback, simply send an e-mail to feedback@packtpub.com, and mention the book title via the subject of your message.

If there is a book that you need and would like to see us publish, please send us a note in the **SUGGEST A TITLE** form on www.packtpub.com or e-mail suggest@packtpub.com.

If there is a topic that you have expertise in and you are interested in either writing or contributing to a book, see our author guide on www.packtpub.com/authors.

Customer support

Now that you are the proud owner of a Packt book, we have a number of things to help you to get the most from your purchase.

Errata

Although we have taken every care to ensure the accuracy of our content, mistakes do happen. If you find a mistake in one of our books—maybe a mistake in the text or the code—we would be grateful if you would report this to us. By doing so, you can save other readers from frustration and help us improve subsequent versions of this book. If you find any errata, please report them by visiting http://www.packtpub.com/support, selecting your book, clicking on the **errata submission form** link, and entering the details of your errata. Once your errata are verified, your submission will be accepted and the errata will be uploaded on our website, or added to any list of existing errata, under the Errata section of that title. Any existing errata can be viewed by selecting your title from http://www.packtpub.com/support.

Piracy

Piracy of copyright material on the Internet is an ongoing problem across all media. At Packt, we take the protection of our copyright and licenses very seriously. If you come across any illegal copies of our works, in any form, on the Internet, please provide us with the location address or website name immediately so that we can pursue a remedy.

Please contact us at copyright@packtpub.com with a link to the suspected pirated material.

We appreciate your help in protecting our authors, and our ability to bring you valuable content.

Questions

You can contact us at questions@packtpub.com if you are having a problem with any aspect of the book, and we will do our best to address it.

Instant Edublogs

Welcome to *Instant Edublogs*. This book will provide an introduction to the Edublogs blogging platform.

Introducing Edublogs.org (Must know)

This recipe will describe how to get started with the Edublogs blogging platform.

Getting ready

Edublogs is a blogging platform based on **WordPress**, an extremely robust platform for long form writing and content management. Edublogs customizes this specifically for educators and students, by adding features that will help them to be more effective. Blogging is a vehicle for becoming a truly reflective practitioner, and connecting with other passionate and dedicated educators online. The recipes in this book will take you from setting up the initial blog, to writing regularly, managing content, developing an audience, customizing it with advanced plugins, and developing a personal identity.

To begin writing and managing a blog on Edublogs, we need to do some preplanning. During registration, we choose our blog URL and title. In this case the URL would be `http://mytitle.edublogs.org`, where `mytitle` is replaced with whatever it is that we choose as our title.

Online readers have a tendency to make quick judgments based on first impressions of a website, so it is imperative to make a great first impression. The first two things that make an impact on a reader are the blog URL and title, which is displayed prominently in most themes.

The title of a blog should reflect its purpose. While the idea of purpose will be discussed more fully later in this book, it is helpful to have some ideas in mind for both the URL and the title. Following are some ideas on inspiration for URL ideas:

> ▶ A URL that is reflective of your current teaching assignment, such as grade level or content area. That is, `http://englishteacher.edublogs.org` or `http://4thgrade.edublogs.org`.

> ▶ A URL that is reflective of your specific point of view on education.

> ▶ A URL that reflects something specific to you, or your school, such as your room number.

> ▶ A URL that demonstrates you are going to talk about many different topics in education. Some examples are `http://avenue4learning.com` or `http://educationontheplate.com`.

> ▶ Your name; your name is not going to change often. It makes sense to invest in your personal brand and online reputation. If you take another name, it is possible to change your domain name.

Whatever you choose for your URL, try to have a few backups in mind as well. It is helpful, although not essential, that your title integrates well into your URL. In the last 2 examples, the titles are *Avenue4Learning* and *Education on the Plate*. This makes the blogs easy to identify if they are subscribed to by e-mail or with an RSS reader.

If at some point in your blogging journey, you decide you want to change your URL and/or your focus, it is possible to do so. However, it can be disconcerting for your readership. Our readers subscribe and come back to our blogs because they appreciate, like, or are challenged by what we say. Changing the URL adds an extra step between the readers and what we have to communicate to them. It is wiser, if possible, to have a memorable title and URL that articulates your intent from the start.

How to do it...

Once you have the ideas for your title and URL, the following steps are actually quite simple:

1. When you go to `http://edublogs.org` for the first time, click on the link on the bottom-right that says **Get your free blog now**, as you will see in the following screenshot. Websites are updated frequently, so it is possible that the button may move. However, there should always be a button to create a free account.

2. The username is important as well. When you leave a comment on someone else's blog, your username is displayed. As educators, everything we do publicly needs to be professional. Online reputation is extremely important. Generally, we do not want something silly or irrelevant. Variations on your name or the title of the blog are acceptable; your name may be preferable, as it is possible to run multiple blogs on the same account. The following screenshot shows how your username will be shown with any comments you leave:

LEAVE A COMMENT

Logged in as bedelljason. Logout »

Comment

☐
Notify me of followup comments via e-mail

Submit

3. Lastly, there are different types of accounts in Edublogs. Make sure that you choose **Teacher** as your account type. Unless you are a student, **Teacher** is most likely the best choice. Upgrading your account to Pro is always possible later on. The following screenshot shows the different types of user accounts:

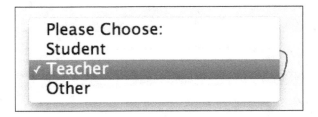

4. Unlike many similar services, you do not get a confirmation e-mail, nor do you have to have to prove your identity by checking your e-mail. This can be helpful when students are registering, but make sure to keep track of your username and password as you will not get a copy in your e-mail.

Choosing a style (Must know)

This recipe will demonstrate how to choose a theme for your blog.

Getting ready

A blog's theme is a very important component of a blog's identity. While we may hope that people will judge our blogs and our writing simply on the merits of our ideas, presentation and perception are vitally important. A blog's theme is one of the things that make each blog unique. The theme is the style—what fonts are used, how objects are situated on a page, what color scheme is applied, and so on. A theme is like a coat of paint. Anytime you want to change the way your blog looks, you can metaphorically add a new coat of paint. Edublogs makes it easy to do this. You just choose one of their themes, and it is instantly applied to your blog.

The following screenshot shows the default theme that Edublogs supplies, called Edublogs Default:

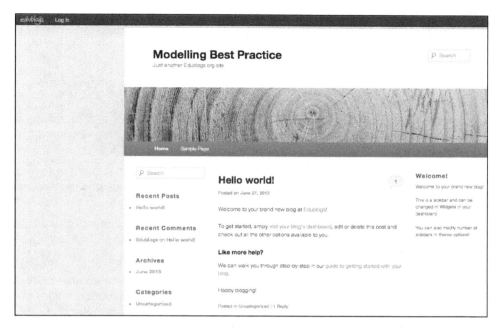

The following is an annotated version of the same screenshot, showing the different pages of the page that a theme can change the style of:

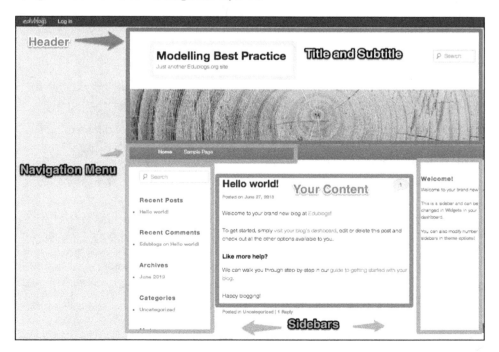

As a web designer and theme developer, there are several questions I always ask clients when we are in the preliminary stages of creating a custom theme.

- What colors or color scheme do you like?
- Are they easy on the eyes? Do they make it is easier to read or are the colors abrasive?
- Do you have a picture in mind that could work as a header image? (The header is the picture and/or text at the very top of the blog. It generally does not change from page to page.)
- What message are you trying to convey with your blog? How does the theme help to convey the central message of your blog? Should it be serious and professional, whimsical and playful, and so on?
- Do you prefer serif fonts (serif fonts have small lines at the end of letters, such as Times New Roman) or sans-serif fonts (such as Arial)?
- Is the format of your blog going to be mostly text, pictures, video, audio, or a mix?
- Do you want to have one or more sidebars? A sidebar is a narrow column to the left or right of the center column where you're content goes. Generally, this is used to display content you are trying to promote, such as posts, links, other blogs, advertisements, and so on. Most blogs have at least one sidebar.

The idea is to get inspiration from other blogs. There is a multitude of blogs available on the Internet on many different subjects. In addition to just looking at the different themes that blogs use, try to get a sense of how their theme interacts with their content.

How to do it...

Hopefully, you are able to answer most of the questions above. You may not be able to, though, especially if you are new to blogging. Following are some things you can do:

1. The next best step is to take some time to look through a lot of different blogs. They do not need to be all teaching blogs, although they can be. They do not need to all even be on Edublogs, although they can be.

2. Sketch out a simple drawing of the layout you want, on paper. Then see if any of the themes are similar.

3. Make a list of the types of things you want in your sidebar, such as lists of posts, calendars, maps, advertisements, links to other blogs, and so on. If you only have three or four, you can easily make a theme with one sidebar work. If you have a lot more, you may want to look at themes with multiple sidebars.

4. Get second opinions from relatives, co-workers, or other bloggers online. A second pair of eyes is always helpful.

How it works...

The first step is to login to the dashboard, or control area, of your blog. There are two ways to do this. First, simply click on the **Log in** button in your sidebar.

Second, you can always go directly to the login page by adding `/wp-login.php` to the end of your blog URL. For example, I created a blog at `http://modellingbestpractice.edublogs.org`. So, to login, I would go to `http://modellingbestpractice.edublogs.org/wp-login.php`.

This is your dashboard. There is a lot going on in the dashboard, arguably much more than in the portion of your blog that is visible to the public. We will get to all of it in time, but for now we need to go to the **Appearance** section, then to **Themes**. Edublogs also has a button to choose a theme, shown in the following screenshot, if this is the first time you are logging in.

You will see a matrix of available themes. Some of the themes are marked as **Edublogs Pro Only**; these are only available if you have a paid account.

You can search the themes if that is preferable to browsing. This is helpful as it allows you to search by colors, the number of columns, the width, and other features. Many of the advanced features are only available on the paid accounts. The following screenshot shows different filters that you can use to search for themes:

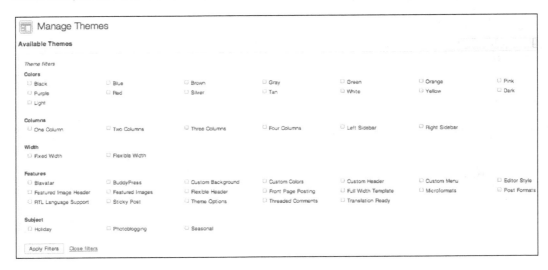

When you find a blog that you like and want to see what it looks like, click on the **Live Preview** button. This will show you what the blog looks like, on your live blog. It does show several configuration options on the left; these are different for each theme. Just click on **Save & Activate** to have the theme applied for readers to see, as seen in the left-hand side column of the following screenshot:

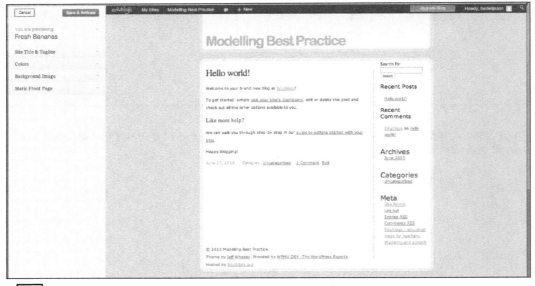

There's more...

Choosing a theme is only the first step. The next step is to choose what type of items, if any, you want in your sidebar(s). Objects such as pictures or links that are displayed in a sidebar are called widgets. There are some already there by default. In the **Appearance** menu, click on **Widgets**.

I only have one sidebar on this blog currently. On the sidebar, Edublogs has added several that are relatively common: **Search**, **Recent Posts**, **Recent Comments**, **Archives**, **Categories**, and **Meta** (the login button), as shown in the following screenshot:

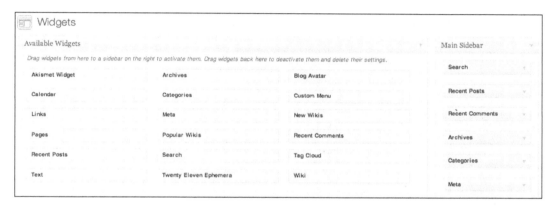

To remove any widgets, just click on the down arrow and then **Delete**. As this is a new blog, I do not have any categories or archives yet, so I'll remove them. I also want to drag the **Links** widget from the **Available Widgets** section over to my sidebar. This will let me specify other blogs that I want to promote. Always think about how the widgets you choose will impact the look of the site and how it would feel to the reader. It is fairly common to add far too many widgets, and thus make the blog look and feel cluttered.

Navigating your dashboard (Must know)

This recipe will introduce the Edublogs dashboard, and how to use it to manage a blog.

Getting ready

The dashboard is the control center of a blog. The dashboard can look a tad overwhelming at first glance. However, it is very logical. Every tool or button on the dashboard corresponds directly to part of the blog that the user can see or interact with. We navigate the dashboard through the menu on the left side of the page. The following screenshot shows the navigation pane of the **Dashboard**:

Edublogs is built on the WordPress platform. WordPress is a free, open source blogging platform used by millions globally. When a software is open source, it signifies that it is free for others to use, add to, or modify. WordPress is an extremely robust platform. It is used on everything from personal blogs, to professional blogs such as *TechCrunch*, that have immense traffic and readership.

Most of the buttons here are part of the core of WordPress, although there are several that Edublogs added specifically to address the needs of the education market.

The **My Class, Wikis, Subscriptions, Stats,** and **Forums** buttons are all additional features that Edublogs has added to WordPress. They have outstanding potential, although if you are just beginning blogging, they are most likely not the features you will need every day. **Plugins** and most of the **Tools** options are also only available to users with a Pro account.

How to do it...

Once we look at the buttons that are left, it becomes much simpler. The **Settings** button is extremely important, although it is used relatively rarely after initial setup. The options that determine how a blog can operate are described in the following section:

1. The **Settings | General** tab has several important options. Here the blog's title and tagline can be modified. The tagline is particularly important as it is shown prominently on most themes, but is not set up during initial registration. In addition, the Timezone must be set for your blog posts to be properly dated.

2. The **Settings | Reading** page dictates how your readers see the content that you create. It lets you adjust the number of posts per page, and the visibility of the site, which can be useful if you are blogging with young students. Another useful feature is the ability to have the home page of your blog not show the blog posts. For example, on the blog for my consulting company, the home page shows an introduction to the services I offer, whereas the blog posts show on another dedicated page. This is not the only way to set up a blog, but it is useful depending on what you are trying to accomplish. The following screenshot shows the important settings in this section:

Front page displays	⦿ Your latest posts
	○ A static page (select below)
	Front page: — Select — ⬍
	Posts page: — Select — ⬍
Blog pages show at most	10 posts
Syndication feeds show the most recent	10 items
For each article in a feed, show	⦿ Full text
	○ Summary
Site Visibility	⦿ Allow search engines to index this site
	○ Discourage search engines from indexing this site
	Note: Neither of these options blocks access to your site — it is up to search engines to honor your request.

3. The **Settings | Discussion** page is another page that is very important. Comments are the lifeblood of a blog, and the **Discussion** page controls how comments work on the site. There are two options here of note. The first is the opportunity to receive an e-mail whenever someone leaves a comment; this is helpful when you are trying to respond quickly and build a sense of community among your readers. The second has to do with moderation. Comment moderation has different levels; you can leave your blog open so that anyone can leave a comment on a post, or restrict it so that no one can leave a comment until you approve what they have written. It becomes even more important if you blog with students, as teachers are entrusted with protecting children from inappropriate interactions online.

4. It is prudent to choose these settings before publicizing your blog; readers expect a consistent experience, and it is disruptive to be making changes to the way that your blog operates on a regular basis.

How it works...

There are three sections that most users will need to go to regularly: **Posts**, **Pages**, and **Comments**. Before continuing, an understanding of the difference between a post and a page is required. A page is a static page on the blog. A common example on most blogs is the **About** page, where a biography or a description of the site would go. A post is the heart of a blog. Posts are the bulk of the content that you create on a blog, and they all go on the blog page (usually just the main page of your blog) in reverse chronological order, with the newest one at the top of the page.

In Edublogs, you create and manage pages and posts in exactly the same way. To add a new post, navigate to **Posts | Add New**. To add a new page, navigate to **Pages | Add New**.

The new post window is fairly straightforward. Add a title and then type your post as you would in a word processing program. The following screenshot shows the **Add New Post** window. We will be going into more depth in the recipe on managing content.

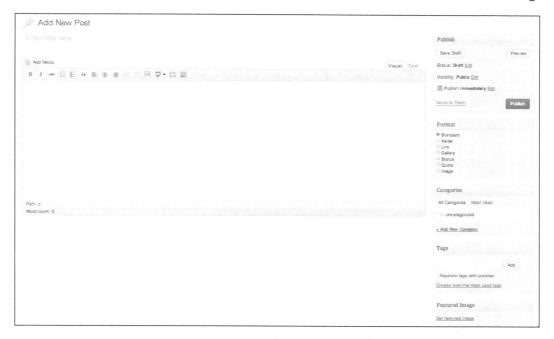

Finding your niche (Must know)

This recipe will illustrate how to find one's place in the blogging community.

Getting ready

It has almost become a cliché that the best writing comes from personal experience. However, there is truth to the saying when it comes to blogging. The educational blogging community is vast; blogging in general even more so. To be heard, what we offer needs to be differentiated from what is already generally available. There are many good questions to be asked.

- ▸ Why am I an authority on this subject?
- ▸ Why would readers want to read about this topic from my perspective?
- ▸ How is what I am offering different from what is already available?

How to do it...

Looking at these questions, there are three things that stand out to differentiate your blog—your experience, knowledge, and voice, explained in the following section:

1. Experience is arguably the most important. Regardless of our position—elementary teacher, secondary teacher, administrator, technologist, and so on—our experiences are different than anyone else's. Our students, our colleagues, and our interactions with them are unique. Those experiences allow us to both illustrate important points, and give the reader an avenue to feel as though he or she has a personal connection to us as writers.

2. Knowledge and experience are interrelated. For content area teachers, knowledge of a specific subject is often vast and intimate. For elementary teachers, knowledge of pedagogy and child development is paramount. Sharing this knowledge and how it relates to our experiences—in other words, how we apply our knowledge to help improve the lives of our students and colleagues—helps create an experience for the reader that is intrinsically unique. In addition, it is helpful to look at what we can offer that others cannot. What, from our knowledge and experience, is unique?

3. Thinking back to my days as a high school language arts teacher, voice was often a difficult, abstract idea for students to grasp. Voice is the style with which someone writes; if two people write a paper on the same topic, using the same facts, what makes those papers different is voice, the individual style of the author.

Your voice may appear indistinct, especially if, when starting your blog, you have not written regularly in some time. Do not worry. As you begin to write regularly, and it becomes a habit, the brain adapts, and you develop more facility at it. An interesting occurrence happens for most bloggers. The more that they write, the more distinct their voice, opinions, and topical choices become. In a sense, voice will develop organically over time, and you will eventually find your niche through trial and error, determining what you enjoy writing about, and seeing what posts readers look at the most. The process, however, can be sped up by considering these ideas—experience, knowledge, and voice—early and often in your blogging journey.

How it works...

To help figure out our own perspective, it can help to see examples of other bloggers with authentic, distinct voices and perspectives. These are educational bloggers who have large followings and specific perspectives. Not all of them use Edublogs as their blogging platform.

▶ **Dr. Kevin D. Washburn** (http://clerestorylearning.com): Kevin is an educational consultant and former teacher who writes often about the intersection of learning and neurology. How does understanding the brain inform teaching practice?

▶ **Dr. Michael Doyle, M.D.** (http://doyle-scienceteach.blogspot.com): Michael is a former medical doctor and currently a high school teacher who writes about engaging students authentically with biology.

- **Jose Vilson** (`http://thejosevilson.com`): Jose is a middle school math teacher and teacher coach who looks at the influence of culture and society on education. He deals with topics that others shy away from, in a straightforward and honest way.
- **Ira Socol** (`http://speedchange.blogspot.com`): Ira is an educator and activist who has a keen eye for finding out ways that the educational system is discriminating against students, and finding ways to provide new learning opportunities.
- **John T. Spencer** (`http://www.educationrethink.com`): John is a middle school ELL teacher. John has extremely varied writings across several blogs. He has a great ability to provide immediately applicable insights through personal reflection.

These authors have a few things in common. They are all great writers—several even have published educational and/or fictional books—and they all have very strong opinions. Their readers could likely read a post and identify them as the author without being told who wrote it. That is an invaluable asset.

There's more...

When I started my blogging journey several years ago, I had no idea what I was really doing. I did not know what I wanted to write about. I wrote generally about education. Both my readership and my purpose were lacking.

Eventually, I figured out what I personally was most interested in—effective ways to integrate technology. I was able to write about this authentically, from my own experiences as an English teacher, a high school library media specialist, an elementary library media specialist, and a district technology coordinator. Even though my circumstances changed, I had a theme from which to build.

The following were a few things that I wanted to do:

- I wanted to get feedback on my ideas and lessons
- I wanted to post lessons that integrate technology
- I wanted to review new tools, both software and hardware, to determine their applicability in education
- I wanted to write to crystallize my own thoughts on technology's role in education, assessment, innovative pedagogy, and professional development

The more I explored these topics, the more distinct my blog became. At the same time, my readership increased. By writing about my personal passion in education, my blog became more worthwhile to me personally, as well as to my readers. Also, having specific goals allows you to keep your blog focused. While it can be tempting to write about any diverse topics, the most successful blogs are usually focused and have a driving theme and purpose.

Committing to a writing schedule (Should know)

This recipe will describe how to provide a steady and predictable stream of content to your readers.

Getting ready

When designing websites and applications, one of the ideas that developers spend a lot of time focusing on, is trying to develop habits in the people they are targeting. It is neither easy nor simple to develop or change someone else's habits. However, there is something that you can do to help your users—commit to a predictable writing schedule.

There are several criteria necessary for developing the habit in the readers to continually check of a blog:

▶ A steady stream of quality, of new content

▶ A predictable stream of quality, of new content

▶ Mechanisms for alerting readers, current and new, of new content

Mechanisms for alerting readers of content are varied, and include RSS and social media These will be described in more detail in *Extending your reach with social Media (Should know)*. The first two points are completely in the writer's control.

A blog only remains relevant as long as it is producing new content. Generally, after you write for some time, there will be several posts that regularly have high numbers of readers from searches, direct links (bookmarks or search results), and social media, but the majority of views for most writers is on their newest content. Without new content posted regularly, readership will dry up.

In addition, it is helpful to have a regular schedule for when you will publish new posts. This does not have to be a specific time; it does not need to be written on your website. However, there cannot be an expectation that readers will regularly, habitually check to see if new content has been posted.

There are any number of schedules that could potentially work; it depends on the time you have available, your style, your subject, and your personal schedule. Following are a few examples of successful blogs with different schedules:

▶ Tom Whitby, an educational consultant and professor, posts usually about once per week. The difference is that his posts are quite long and very thorough. Posts like that take a significant time investment to write, and readers do not expect new content of that length so quickly. He is available at `http://tomwhitby.wordpress.com`.

> ▶ Richard Byrne, a teacher and consultant from the immensely popular *Free Tech 4 Teachers* blog, writes several posts per day. He tends to write them in advance and schedules them to post at different times during the day. Writing about different educational tools allows him to write posts that are engaging and relatively brief, generally 2-4 paragraphs. His blog can be found at `http://www.freetech4teachers.com`.

Richard and Tom are on different ends of the scheduling spectrum, but they both have loyal readers. These serve as illustrations that giving readers an expectation of when to expect new content, combined with providing high quality content, helps readers to be confident that checking on the site again will be worth their time.

Keeping to a schedule like Richard's, with several posts per day, is likely not something most can commit to, especially when just beginning to blog. There are options, though.

One schedule that has worked well for me in the past is trying to write 2-3 posts per week, depending on the time and circumstances. When I was trying to write two posts per week, I would publish a shorter post on Wednesday and a longer post on the weekend. When I was trying to write three posts per week, I would publish two short posts during the week, usually on Monday and Wednesday, and a longer post on the weekends.

It may take some time and trial and error to find a schedule that works for you. Once you do, try to stick to it as a minimum for what you write as a courtesy to your readers.

How to do it...

Developing a writing schedule that you can really commit to takes forethought, trial, and error.

1. The first step is to analyze your current schedule and see when you have time to write. For example, I am a technology coordinator for a school working 6 A.M. to 3 P.M. during the week, and often do consulting and programming work in the evening. The most that I can usually write in a week is two shorter posts, one in the evening after work, and one in the morning before work, and one more in-depth post on the weekends.

2. Try to follow the schedule for at least 2-3 weeks. It's hard to evaluate a schedule based on the strength of one week. If it works, fabulous. If not, that's fine. Analyze what went wrong. Did you attempt to write too many posts in one week? Did you try to write at times that did not work well due to work, obligations, lack of energy, and so on? Create a new schedule based on your analysis.

3. Once you find a schedule that works for you, the next step is to work at it until it becomes habitual, an essential part of your routine. One way to help you do that is to put repeated reminders in your calendar. Once blogging is integrated into your routine, it becomes much easier to maintain momentum; it no longer feels like something that you must make time for.

Managing content (Must know)

This recipe provides details about managing different types of content.

Getting ready

Content in Edublogs can take many different forms—posts, pages, uploaded media, and embedded media. The first step needs to be developing an understanding of what each of these types of content are, and how they fit into the Edublogs framework.

 ▸ **Pages**: Pages are generally static content, such as an About or a Frequently Asked Questions page.

 ▸ **Posts**: Posts are the content that is continually updated on a blog. When you write an article, it is referred to as a post.

 ▸ **Media** [uploaded]: Edublogs has a media manager that allows you to upload pictures, videos, audio files, and other files that readers would be able to interact with or download.

 ▸ **Media** [embedded]: Embedded media is different than internal media in that it is not stored on your Edublogs account. If you record a video and upload it, the video resides on your website and is considered internal to that website. If you want to add a YouTube video, a Prezi presentation, a slideshow, or any content that actually resides on another website, that is considered embedding.

How to do it...

Posts and pages are very similar, as was introduced in *Navigating your dashboard (Must know)*. When you click on the **Pages** link on the left navigation column, if you are just beginning, you will see an empty list or the Sample Page that Edublogs provides. However, this page will show a list of all of the pages that you have written, as shown in the following screenshot:

1. Click on any column header (**Title**, **Author**, Comments, and **Date**) to sort the pages by that criterion. A page can be any of several types: **Published** (anyone can see), **Drafts**, **Private**, Password Protected, or in the **Trash**. You can filter by those pages as well. You will only see the types of pages that you are currently using. For example, in the following screenshot, I have 3 Draft pages. If I had none, **Drafts** would not show as an option.

2. When you hover over a page, you are provided with several options, such as **Edit**, **Quick Edit**, **Trash**, and **View**.

   - **View**: This option shows you the actual live post, the same way that a reader would see it.

   - **Trash**: This deletes the page.

   - **Edit**: This brings you back to the main editing screen, where you can change the actual body of the page.

   - **Quick Edit**: This allows you to change some of the main options of the post: **Title**, **Slug** (the end of the URL to access the page), **Author**, if the page has a parent, and if it should be published. The following screenshot demonstrates these options:

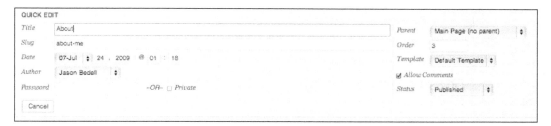

How it works...

Everything above about **Pages** also applies to **Posts**. **Posts**, though, have several additional options. It's also more common to use the additional options to customize **Posts** than **Pages**.

Right away, hovering over **Posts**, it shows two new links: **Categories** and **Tags**. These tools are optional, and serve the dual purpose of aiding the author by providing an organizational structure, and helping the reader to find posts more effectively. A Category is usually very general; on one of my educational blogs, I limit my categories to a few: technology integration, assessment, pedagogy, and lessons. If I happen to write a post that does not fit, I do not categorize it. Tags are becoming ubiquitous in many applications and operating systems.

They provide an easy way to browse a store of information thematically. On my educational blog, I have over 160 tags. On one post about Facebook's new advertising system, I added the following tags: Digital Literacy, Facebook, Privacy. Utilizing tags can help you to see trends in your writing and makes it much easier for new readers to find posts that interest them, and regular readers to find old posts that they want to re-reference.

Let's take a look at some of the advanced features. When adding or editing a post, the following features are all located on the right-hand side column:

- **Publish**: The **Publish** box is necessary any time you want to remove your Post (or Page) from the draft stage, and allow readers to be able to see it. Most new bloggers simply click on **Publish/Update** when they are done writing a Post, which works fine. It is limited though. People often find that there are certain times of day that result in higher readership. If you click on **Edit** next to **Publish Immediately**, you can choose a date and time to schedule the publication. In addition, the **Visibility** line also allows you to set a Post as private, password protected, or always at the top of the page (if you have a post you particularly want to highlight, for example).

- **Format**: Most of the time, changing the format is not necessary, particularly if you run a normal, text driven blog. However, different formats lend themselves to different types of content. For example, if publishing a picture as a Post, as is often done on the microblogging site Tumblr, choosing **Image** would format the post more effectively.

- **Categories**: Click on **+ Add New Category**, or check any existing categories to append them to the Post.

- **Tags**: Type any tags that you want to use, separated by commas (such as writing, blogging, Edublogs).

- **Featured Image**: Uploading and choosing a feature image adds a thumbnail image, to provide a more engaging browsing experience for the viewer.

All of these features are optional, but they are useful for improving the experience, both for yourself and your readers.

There's more...

While for most people, the heart of a blog is the actual writing that they do. Media serves help to both make the experience more memorable and engaging, as well as to illustrate a point more effectively than text would alone. Media is anything other than text that a user can interact with; primarily, it is video, audio, or pictures. As teachers know, not everyone learns ideally through a text-based medium; media is an important part of engaging readers just as it is an important part of engaging students.

There are a few ways to get media into your posts. The first is through the **Media Library**. On a free account, space is limited to 32 MB, a relatively small account. Pro accounts get 10 GB of space.

Click on **Media** from the navigation menu on the left; it brings up the library. This will have a list of your media, similar to that which is used for Posts and Pages. To add media, simply click on **Add New** and choose an image, audio file, or video from your computer. This will then be available to any post or page to use. The following screenshot shows the **Media Library** page:

If you are already in a post, you have even more options. Click on the **Add Media** button above the text editor, as shown in the following screenshot:

Following are some of the options you have to embed media:

> ▶ **Insert Media**: This allows you to directly upload a file or choose one from the **Media Library**.

> ▶ **Create Gallery**: Creating a gallery allows you to create a set of images that users can browse through.

- ► **Set Featured Image:** As described above, set a thumbnail image representative of the post.

- ► **Insert from URL:** This allows you to insert an image by pasting in the direct URL. Make sure you give attribution, if you use someone else's image.

- ► **Insert Embed Code:** Embed code is extremely helpful. Many sites provide embed code (often referred to as share code) to allow people to post their content on other websites. One of the most common examples is adding a YouTube video to a post. The following screenshot is from the **Share** menu of a YouTube video. Copying the code provided and pasting it into the **Insert Embed Code** field will put the YouTube video right in the post, as shown in the following screenshot. This is much more effective than just providing a link, because readers can watch the video without ever having to leave the blog. Embedding is an Edublogs Pro feature only.

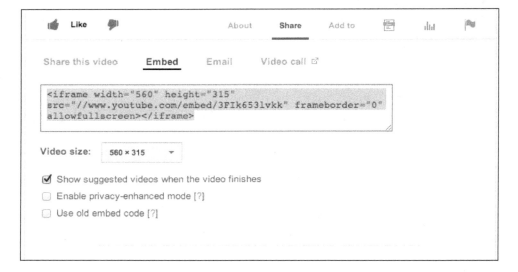

Utilizing media effectively can dramatically improve the experience for your readers.

Growing an audience organically (Should know)

This recipe details strategies for investing in and growing your readership.

Getting ready

The most common analogy often used to describe a blog is that of an online journal. True reflective practice is personal; it often reveals one's mistakes more often than it basks in successes. So why, in a time when teachers are attacked and vilified from all sides, would anyone want to put their personal thoughts and experiences out there for anyone to see? Would it not be better to just write and reflect privately? While it is certainly possible that many will indeed come to such a conclusion, most teachers that have been blogging for any period of time can attest to the value that it has had for them personally. Following are the four reasons which show that publicly reflecting on a blog is more worthwhile to many than taking a safer alternative:

- ▶ Accountability
- ▶ Transparency
- ▶ Community
- ▶ Validation

Despite the message often sent by politicians and the media, educators want accountability. Most educators do not want to be left alone, to fail or succeed on their own. The knowledge that there is a potential public audience is a cause to carefully consider and craft one's message. After a particularly troubling day or difficult lesson, it is easy to vent. It is not often productive, but it is easy to fall into that routine. However, through my reflective, public writing, I would want to carefully consider what happened. Instead of blaming kids for misbehaving, for example, I will look deeper to try and find the root cause. Perhaps I did not teach the concept well and they were acting out because they were lost. There could have been extenuating circumstances that I was not aware of; instead of assigning blame, I am able to move past it, to try to find a solution. It is both cathartic and productive. Public writing promotes responsibility and accountability in a good and natural way. As with all criticism, and public writing will occasionally engender criticism, there is a choice to get angry, to ignore it, or to explore it and see if the person has a point. By opening up one's writing publicly, we invite a type of criticism that can help us grow.

Many of the administrators and parents I have worked with were very surprised by the level of transparency that I wanted in my classroom. I wanted them to have my lesson plans. I wanted them to be in my classroom regularly. I wanted them to know what I was doing and, more importantly, what the students were doing. Other teachers and administrators can offer great insight on instruction. Parents can offer great insight into the needs of their children. The feedback that can come about as a result of a collaborative transparency is transformational. This is not transparency because the administrators are spying on my classroom. This is transparency that stems from wanting all stakeholders to be truly involved to improve the experience for the students. Blogging is an extension of that. It can offer a window into your world, the world in which your students live.

The longer you blog, the more you get to know your readers, and the more a mutual trusting relationship is built. There is a proportional relationship between how much and how honestly you share, and how well the community develops. The community of readers is here to get to know you and to grow with you. If you are not honest with them, then you erect a barrier and the relationship grows more slowly. Those who have been following my blog since its inception in my second year teaching, know that my greatest difficulty as a teacher was classroom management. I am glad that I was honest about this. I received a lot of feedback on things that I was doing; I've learned and grown much in this area because of the help that I have got from the community. I went from trying to control my classroom to giving up control, by developing a good relationship with the students, giving them choices, and trusting them to make the right decisions; behavior issues became mostly a non-issue. While I still have room to grow in this area, it would have taken far longer for me to progress as far as I have, had not the community helped to show me what I was doing wrong. While I know people who have, I have never had a hostile or an insulting comment. Most people who spend time reading what you have to say about education truly have a desire to both learn and help.

Sometimes, it can feel very lonely in a school, especially when you feel as though you are a minority in terms of trying new approaches, ideas, or techniques in your classroom. This is not to say that few teachers are innovative, but rather speaks to a sense of isolation that many teachers, especially those new to the profession, often feel. Having limited time in the school day to plan and collaborate with others in the building can exacerbate this feeling. I have often worked with great educators; however, there have been times when I wanted to try things that were not yet commonplace in my school. An example is being the only teacher in the school teaching a blended environment. There was not anyone in the school that I could really go to for guidance. Thankfully, some of my readers have been in that situation. They were able to help validate that some of what I was doing was indeed good; this gave me more confidence to keep at what I was doing.

Our readers are the primary way through which our blogs have meaning, develop relevance, and make a difference. We need to consciously invest in our readers so as they invest in us.

How to do it...

Looking at the comments of any blog can show how vibrant its community of readers really is. Comments are the main avenue of communication between author and audience. There are steps that you can take to foster a community where people comment and interact frequently, honestly, and naturally.

1. Make time to comment on other people's blogs. In doing so, you are fostering communication and supporting another blogger/educator. A side effect of supporting others in this fashion is that the author will often check out and comment on your blog. Furthermore, anyone reading that person's post will be exposed to your site and may check it out as well. The community that you are trying to build is extended beyond just your own blog.

2. Create an atmosphere that does not put your opinion above anyone else's. It is your site, but you do not necessarily need to be the expert all the time. If you are the sole expert about what you are writing, then why do you need other people to contribute? Readers need to know that they can make a valuable contribution to the blog, or they will not waste their time.

3. Ask. There is a large difference in the amount and quality of comments when you ask people for help or for their opinion, and when you do not. I will often end my posts with a question because I really want to know what the people reading think. Do they agree or disagree? Why?

4. Be polite. Ideally, your commenters will not always agree with everything you say. Of course, validation is important and helpful, but if everyone agrees, then what is really learned? What impact can be had if no one is moved outside of his comfort zone? So, the longer you blog, the higher the chance that someone will disagree with you. This is a good thing because we can learn through the process of disagreeing. In the event that a commenter is argumentative, try to be polite and positive.

5. Respond often. When I first started blogging, I would respond to every comment. I had my blog setup to e-mail me whenever I receive a comment so that I could reply in a timely fashion. Our readers' time is important, and leaving a question unanswered for days shows a disregard for the value of their time. As the community around a blog develops, the readers will often respond to each other. Foster this; it is the sign of a thriving community.

The more you and your readers are able to interact, the more value everyone, including you, will be able to derive from your blog. So it is definitely worth it to try to create an environment where people are comfortable to comment.

How it works...

Edublogs allows us to setup different levels of moderation. This can be accessed by going to the **Discussion** section in the **Settings** menu.

The default settings from Edublogs are shown in the following screenshot:

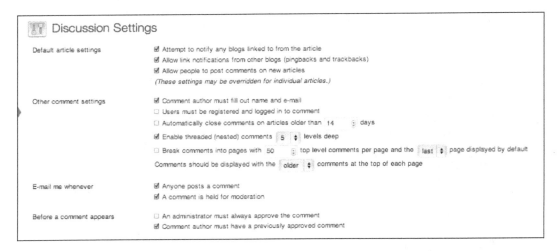

The following are a few settings in particular that I would like to highlight:

- ▶ **Comment author must fill out name and e-mail**: I keep this setting checked, so that it is more likely people will use their real name/online identity.

- ▶ **Users must be registered and logged in to comment**: I keep this unchecked so that I may receive comments from anyone, not just Edublogs users.

- ▶ **Enable threaded (nested) comments**: This allows users to respond to each other's comments, not just to the general posts.

- ▶ **Email me whenever**: I like to keep **Anyone posts a comment** checked, to make sure I respond to comments relatively quickly.

- ▶ **Before a comment appears**: Checking **An administrator must always approve the comment** will hold all comments until you approve them.

- ▶ **Before a comment appears**: Checking **Comment author must have a previously approved comment** will hold a comment if the reader has never had a comment approved before.

There is no way to moderate what works best in every situation. Some writers like to approve every comment so that they can screen comments for appropriateness. I personally assume the best in my readers; I allow all comments without moderation and will remove any that are blatantly inappropriate.

There is a fine line of trust though. If you moderate all comments, be sure to approve comments that you disagree with, as long as they are appropriate. The moment readers realize that an author picks and chooses only certain comments to be approved, that author has lost all credibility, and it is difficult to convince readers to return.

Extending your reach with social media (Should know)

This recipe will show some methods for growing an audience using social media.

Getting ready

There is an interesting conundrum when starting a blog. Those blogs that have vast audiences already have a built-in publicity machine. When a blog like *Lifehacker* (http://lifehacker.com), that likely has followers in the millions, publishes a post, many of its readers will find it interesting and then tell others about it. This perpetuates further, organic growth, as the blog re-engages its audience, and that audience, in turn, brings in more readers. When a new blogger writes a post, who reads it? How do people hear about it? *Lifehacker*, and blogs of similar size and loyalty, have an inherent advantage that a new blogger cannot match. That means that when we write a post, we need to be creative in finding ways to tell people about what we have written. There are any number of ways to do this. One proven way is through creating a personal learning network on social media.

In education, as in most professions, there is a vernacular of sorts, a common terminology that is supposed to unify educators and help them to meet on common grounds. The problem is that new buzzwords seem to come up very often, while others are discarded. It is inherent in education. Everyone has an opinion on education; "experts" come up with new ideas; politicians propose new "reforms." Most of these seem to add to the chaos, but not to progress. So, it is not surprising if you have not heard this term before.

The term **PLN** is an acronym that stands for **personal learning network**. I have heard several variations. Two of the most popular are professional learning network, which seems limiting if you ever want to learn something outside of your immediate profession, and **personal learning environment** (**PLE**), which is often used either interchangeably or with a slightly different meaning than PLN.

The idea and value of a PLN has caused more controversy and debate than I believe it merits. Personal learning networks have always existed, regardless of the terminology around to identify them as such. The word network implies connections; connections can either be to people or resources. The connections are used for learning that applies to you personally. So, in short, your personal learning network is any people or resources that help you to learn.

You already have a personal learning network. We could both teach the same subject, and grade, even at the same school, and have completely different personal learning networks. The beauty of it is that we align ourselves and our resources to maximize our own learning. There will obviously be differences in the depth, range, and quality of different people's personal learning networks. The shift comes when you recognize your network for what it is, analyze its strengths and weaknesses, and then try to make more connections to grow in the areas where your network is not meeting your needs.

In my first year of teaching, my personal learning network really only consisted of my mentor teacher for the first few months. There was no one else that I knew to look to for help, and really no one that I was contributing to. In the spring semester, I started co-planning and meeting with other teachers in my grade level and subject area regularly. This opened me up to a wide range of resources that I had not had access to. These people, along with a few lesson plan sites and some professional literature, were the network of connections that I was using to become a better educator.

As my second year started, I realized that I was not improving as quickly as I needed to in order to best serve my students. The people in my building were wonderful, but they could not provide me with everything I needed. It is impossible, because their skill set, while varied, did not exactly line up with my needs. It was also often limited to meetings before and after school. So, I started to take action to broaden my network.

I started my own blog, and reading the blogs and reflective writings of other educators beyond those in my building. I started following the bookmarks of people in many of the different schools in the district I was in; this way, I had access to many of the great resources they were finding. I started to connect and talk to great teachers and educators all over the world on Twitter and other social networks. I contributed, and still do, as much as I possibly can, but what I got back from the networks was such a great boon. I am a better educator because of it, and I continue to improve because of the connections that I have made.

For me personally, I have found Twitter to be the most useful social network for both sharing my blog and for professional development. Twitter is routinely the most popular referrer (site that users use to find your blog), beating Facebook, Google searches, and more. I have several thousand followers (people who read my posts) on Twitter. That does not make me a Twitter celebrity by any means; however, it does mean that there is a sizeable potential audience. It becomes even bigger if any of those followers retweet (post again) a post that I have written. If they do so, my post is then visible to all of their followers.

There are several people I talk to on Twitter who share their blog posts repeatedly for a few days after writing. There is a line here that we need to be careful not to cross. I make it a point not to tweet a blog post more than twice, usually once in the evening and once in the morning, in any given day. I realize that by limiting it, I am limiting my potential audience. The trade-off is that I do not come off as obnoxious and taking advantage of my followers strictly to garner page views for my blog. In addition, my tweets are more valuable; a smaller percentage of them are focused on marketing, so more of them can be focused on helping others and participating in meaningful discussions. Most educators online are fine with a certain amount of sharing, because they realize we are sharing our blog posts to support and edify the educational community.

How to do it...

Social media is simply any website that is built around social interaction. The two largest social networks for most regions of the world are Facebook and Twitter; they will be discussed here more than other social networks. That said, depending on your specific circumstances, they may not be where you want the bulk of your focus. Marketing through social media is personal; you need to find where you are comfortable, and what works for you. Trying several social networks and tracking analytics to see which sites referred readers to your blog is an effective way to gauge which sites you should pour your energy into. There are education focused social networks like Learnist. There are curation-focused networks like Pinterest and Diigo. There are a lot of photography-centric networks, the largest of which is Instagram. There are video-centric networks like YouTube and Vine.

1. When you write your blog post, post a link to your blog on several networks.

2. Using the **Dashboard**, keep track of which sites send you the most referrals.

3. To make the best use of your time, pick 1-3 networks to invest your time into, and focus on that. It is not necessary to share every post on every possible network. You will see greater dividends with a more focused approach.

4. To be effective on a network requires actively engaging with a network. This is not a quick process. Think about starting a blog. The first time you write a post, there is no one to read it. Twitter, Facebook, and others, are the same way; if you are just creating an account, there is no one there to read your status update, your tweet, and so on.

Try your best to invest in relationships and provide real value to people. This helps you to develop a reputation as someone who is both helpful and who possesses expertise. There is a reciprocal benefit. As you invest in relationships, you learn from other people, and those people become much more likely to read and think about your writing.

How it works...

A discerning reader will have noticed a problem. Social media is only useful to help alleviate the issue of blog readership if someone already has a following on a social network. How does one go about developing followers? The answer is deceptively simple: provide value, and invest in relationships.

If you are writing an educational blog, it is safe to assume that your audience is one of the following:

- ▶ Teachers, administrators, and other educators
- ▶ Students and parents
- ▶ People considering going into education
- ▶ Politicians interested in reforming education

People in these groups need to be able to see a correlation between talking to you and making a real difference. For teacher-readers, can they take what you are saying and help their students? For parent-readers, can they take what you are saying and help their children? For politicians, can what you are saying inform their policies?

Creating value takes time. Quality content on your blog is a wonderful first step. When you talk to someone on Twitter, or tweet them, people will often check out your profile, view your blog, and see if you are the type of person they are interested in following. Some great blog posts help to set you up as someone who is an authority on some aspect of education.

Another way to create value is to find people talking about education and participate in those discussions. Twitter, more than any other network, allows people to easily find those who share similar interests. It can be helpful, when developing your online identity, to try to secure the same username on multiple networks. My personal blog URL is the same as my Twitter username; this helps to build a reputation and makes discovery easier. Often, this is done through the use of **hashtags**—a hashtag is a search term preceded by a # symbol. These are supremely useful. If someone writes a tweet with the hashtag #education, anyone in the world can see the tweet when they search for that hashtag. Jerry Blumengarten, an outstanding retired educator who runs the Cybrary Man website (http://cybraryman.com) and tries to help other educators on Twitter and at educational conferences, has a listing of many of the most used educational hashtags, and when they are most active. This listing is available at http://cybraryman.com/edhashtags.html. #edchat (general education), #tlchat (teacher-librarian focused), and #edtechchat are some of my favorites at the moment. The more that I participate in these chats, the more other participants find my ideas of value, and are more likely to both follow me and read my blog.

There's more...

I would like to list some of the reasons why I am such a passionate advocate of Twitter. In the few years that I have been using it, I have seen immense benefit and really have become a better teacher. I follow about 2,000 educators and am followed by close to 4,000. I give back to the community whenever I can, but with a ratio of 4000:1, I always receive much more than I have given. The vastness and diversity of experience lets me see things from a perspective that I would not otherwise have had. It was on Twitter that I got the support and the necessary help to write this book. Many times this year when I needed help on a lesson or finding a tool, the educators on Twitter helped me not only with much better ideas, but by providing them more quickly than I could find. Twitter has been better than any single professional development tool because I am able to talk about ideas that are current and relevant to my profession on a daily basis. Furthermore, I have even seen a material benefit. Twitter has allowed me to connect with other educators in meaningful ways outside of the Internet. Twitter has enriched both my personal and professional life.

What can you share on Twitter? Having friends and family on Twitter or other social networks can definitely make it more enjoyable. However, the suggestions here are limited to those that deal with education. They are merely some ideas that have worked well for many teachers, and are not binding or all-encompassing.

- ▶ Share what your students are working on right now.
- ▶ Brag about your students. It is good to be proud of them when they accomplish something.
- ▶ Share your struggles. With all the teachers on Twitter, someone has been where you are, and no one will judge you for having trouble.
- ▶ Share ideas—lesson plans, tools, assessment strategies.
- ▶ Ask for help when you are stuck.
- ▶ Share resources or links that you find online.
- ▶ Give credit to someone when he or she has a good idea. Sharing the ideas of others is welcome; this kind of collaboration helps build up other writers, and benefits your readers. However, attribution to the original writer must be given, preferably with a link to the original post.
- ▶ Conversely, you can gain much from using what others are saying.
- ▶ Gain confidence in your students. Find out how much they are capable of, from seeing what other students are doing.
- ▶ Share the accomplishments of other teachers and students whom you have impacted.
- ▶ Help another teacher. Everyone struggles at some point; there may be someone that you are in a unique position to help because of your knowledge and experience.

- ► Find new ideas, plans, strategies, and so on.
- ► Get help tailored to your needs.
- ► Find great new resources from other teachers.
- ► Be publicly given credit when you have a good idea.

There is an intentional pattern in this. Humans in general thrive on relationships. Educators in particular are in the business of relationships. It may have become a cliché, but there is truth to the saying that students do not care what you know until they know that you care about them. Other educators may differ in background and experience, but most are here because they genuinely believe that they can learn something that can help their students, and possibly help students' interests. If you approach social networking with the goal of helping all students, then you will be both enriched and a help to others. In the process, the audience of your blog will grow proportionally to the relationships you are a part of and the value you provide.

Using plugins for greater engagement (Become an expert)

This recipe will detail some of the advanced plugins that can be utilized with Edublogs Pro accounts.

Getting ready

Several times in this book, there have been certain limitations put on Edublogs free users. This and the remaining recipes deal with advanced features that are only available to Edublogs Pro customers. If you want to upgrade any of your Edublogs blogs to Pro, simply go to `https://edublogs.org/pro-upgrade/`. It is about $5 per month, although purchasing in greater blocks of time reduces the per month cost. It is perfectly fine to peruse these next recipes, but if you want to follow along on your own blog, you will need to upgrade for at least 1 month ($4.95 at the time of this writing). As an added bonus, there are tons of features that have been mentioned previously that will also become available to you, such as premium themes, extra space for media uploads, and more.

So, what exactly is a plugin? Edublogs is based on the extremely powerful WordPress blogging platform. WordPress is itself open source, which means that the source code that makes the program work is free for anyone to look at or modify. Edublogs is one of a number of sites that have customized WordPress to offer services that it was not designed for. Edublogs has made changes specific to the educational market, by adding features such as creating classes or **Wikis**.

Modifying the core of WordPress, as Edublogs has, is only one of the ways that we, as authors, benefit from WordPress being open source. Another way that developers have improved on WordPress is by adding or changing specific features; they do this through custom code called a plugin. Edublogs has taken some of the best plugins and made them available to Pro users. Some are relatively simple and superficial, while others add a lot more power and customizability to a blog.

How to do it...

Plugins can be complex and powerful; most, though, were created to fill a specific need. This recipe will look at several plugins, but it is not exhaustive. Edublogs can also add more at any time as they determine others would be useful for their users.

1. To access the list of plugins, click on the **Installed Plugins** button from the **Plugins** menu on the left-hand side.

2. Following is a screenshot of the plugins that Edublogs offers at the time of this writing. Not included in the image is the extremely popular **Akismet** plugin, which blocks spam, and which Edublogs has automatically turned on by default on all blogs, premium or not.

Plugin	Description
3D Rotating Tag Cloud (WP Cumulus) Activate	Creates a beautiful rotating and animated representation of all your tags and categories which visitors can then click on to visit archives. Once activated just drag and edit the new widget in Appearance -> Widgets.
Accept PayPal Donations Activate	Easily add a PayPal donate button to your blog's sidebar with this plugin. Once activated configure under Settings > WP PayPal Payment.
AddThis Social Bookmarking Activate	Help your visitor promote your site! Once activated go to Settings > AddThis Social Share and enable to display on your posts or go to Appearance > Widgets and add the AddThis Social Share Widget to your sidebar.
Classbadges Student Badges Activate	The ClassBadges plugin allows any student registered on ClassBadges.com to share badges in their public folder on a WordPress blog.
Compfight Activate	Quickly find the perfect Creative Commons licensed photo every time. Add them to your blog posts with the proper attribution every time with just one click!
Contact Form Activate	A straightforward contact form - allows visitors to your blog to send you an email. After activating visit Settings -> Contact Form.
DOGO Content Widget Activate	Enable widgets to display engaging content from one or more DOGO websites: Expose students to current events with the DOGOnews widget, an award-wining source of content for Common Core State Standards ELA, Science & Social Studies. Encourage reading with book reviews and peer recommendations with the DOGObooks widget. And for fun, share movie reviews by kids with the DOGOmovies widget.
FeedBurner FeedSmith Activate	Originally authored by Steve Smith, this plugin detects all ways to access your original WordPress feeds and redirects them to your FeedBurner feed so you can track every possible subscriber.
Footnotes Activate	Elegant and easy to use footnotes - simply type them inline in your post in square brackets like this: [1. This is a footnote.] Each footnote must have a number followed by a period and a space and then the actual footnote.
Formidable Activate	Quickly and easily create drag-and-drop forms
Google Maps Activate	Easily embed, customize, and use Google maps on your WordPress site - in posts, pages or as an easy to use widget, display local images and let your site visitors get directions in seconds.

The other plugins available at the time of this writing are shown in the following screenshot:

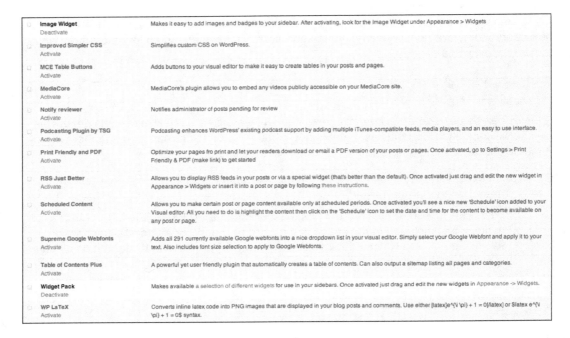

Image Widget Deactivate	Makes it easy to add images and badges to your sidebar. After activating, look for the Image Widget under Appearance > Widgets
Improved Simpler CSS Activate	Simplifies custom CSS on WordPress.
MCE Table Buttons Activate	Adds buttons to your visual editor to make it easy to create tables in your posts and pages.
MediaCore Activate	MediaCore's plugin allows you to embed any videos publicly accessible on your MediaCore site.
Notify reviewer Activate	Notifies administrator of posts pending for review
Podcasting Plugin by TSG Activate	Podcasting enhances WordPress' existing podcast support by adding multiple iTunes-compatible feeds, media players, and an easy to use interface.
Print Friendly and PDF Activate	Optimize your pages fro print and let your readers download or email a PDF version of your posts or pages. Once activated, go to Settings > Print Friendly & PDF (make link) to get started
RSS Just Better Activate	Allows you to display RSS feeds in your posts or via a special widget (that's better than the default). Once activated just drag and edit the new widget in Appearance > Widgets or insert it into a post or page by following these instructions.
Scheduled Content Activate	Allows you to make certain post or page content available only at scheduled periods. Once activated you'll see a nice new 'Schedule' icon added to your Visual editor. All you need to do is highlight the content then click on the 'Schedule' icon to set the date and time for the content to become available on any post or page.
Supreme Google Webfonts Activate	Adds all 291 currently available Google webfonts into a nice dropdown list in your visual editor. Simply select your Google Webfont and apply it to your text. Also includes font size selection to apply to Google Webfonts.
Table of Contents Plus Activate	A powerful yet user friendly plugin that automatically creates a table of contents. Can also output a sitemap listing all pages and categories.
Widget Pack Deactivate	Makes available a selection of different widgets for use in your sidebars. Once activated just drag and edit the new widgets in Appearance -> Widgets.
WP LaTeX Activate	Converts inline latex code into PNG images that are displayed in your blog posts and comments. Use either [latex]e^{\i \pi} + 1 = 0[/latex] or \$latex e^{\i \pi} + 1 = 0\$ syntax.

3. Notice that in the screenshots each plugin, depending on whether it is already in use, has a link that says either **Activate** or **Deactivate**. You simply click on the **Activate** button to turn a plugin on.

Plugins can affect any area of Edublogs. Some change the way your dashboard works by adding functionality, and others change what readers see or the way that they interact with the blog.

How it works...

Clicking on **Activate** for some plugins turns them on and sets them up completely; for others, it enables them so that you can customize them or use them when you need them. To help illustrate how different types of plugins work, the following looks at a few:

▶ **3D Rotating Tag Cloud**: Clicking on **Activate** enables a new type of widget that you can add to your sidebar. It takes all the tags you use and, instead of the normal list layout, shows them in an aesthetically pleasing 3D image.

▶ **Accept Paypal Donations**: If you want, it is possible to ask your readers to support what you do via PayPal. If you do so, make sure you are providing real value. Asking for donations can offend some readers. Clicking on **Activate** adds a new entry in the **Settings** menu—**WP PayPal Payment**. From this page, you can customize your donation message and payment options. This would add a widget to your blog's sidebar. The following screenshot shows the settings to the plugin:

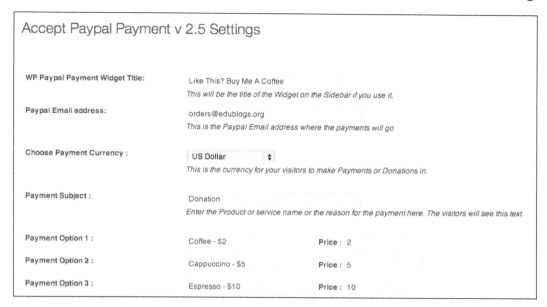

- ► **MCE Table Buttons**: This is different than the preceding; instead of affecting the widgets, this adds buttons to the sidebar. Specifically, it adds a set of buttons and a menu to the text editor, to make working with tables much easier, as shown in the following screenshot:

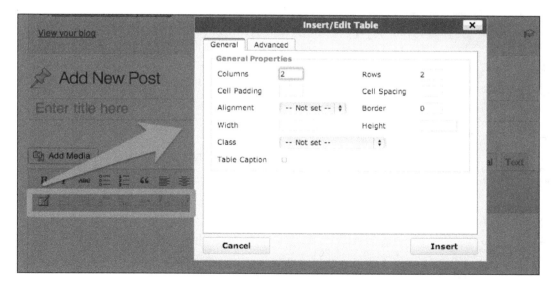

▶ **Supreme Google Webfonts**: Google has a repository of several hundred fonts. Activating this allows you to choose them from the text editor when typing. Use caution, though, as the developer admits it may add a few seconds to the time it takes to load the page.

There's more...

The plugins range in complexity from the simple (for example, the Webfonts plugin mentioned in the previous section simply adds a font drop-down menu) to much more complicated. The **Contact Form** plugin is somewhat more complicated and involved.

After activating the plugin, go to the **Settings** menu and click on the **Contact Form** entry. Let's create a simple contact form, so that readers can get in touch with us outside of just through comments. If readers have questions about a topic that would not be relevant in a comment, it is helpful to provide another avenue for them to contact.

Add your e-mail address (this is not viewable to the readers). I also like to change the message that readers receive after filling out the form. Instead of the default **Thanks for your comments!** message, I would change it to something more specific, such as `Thank you! I will send a reply in 2-3 days`. The following screenshot shows the configuration options for the plugin:

Contact Form Options

E-mail Address:

This address is where the email will be sent to. Multiple recipients can be separated by a comma.

Legend:

Contact Form

This is a legend for your contact form. If you do not wish to have a legend, just leave it blank.

Subject Line:

Contact Form Results

If you would like a list box to select an option from on the form, input your information delimited by a '|' (example: Website | Plugin | Help)

☑ Check this box to allow users to include a Subject line. It will be concatenated to your default subject line. This will be the subject of the email.

Challenge Question

What is your challenge question?

2 + 2 =

This is a question asked to the contact form user to see if they are human.

Correct response:

4

This is the exact response to the challenge question.

☐ Check this box if you don't care if the user types the response with the correct case sensitivity.

Messages

Success Message:

Thanks for your comments!

When the form is successfully submitted, this is the message the user will see.

Error Message:

Please fill in the required fields

If the user skips a required field, this is the message he will see.
You can apply CSS to this text by wrapping it in `<p style="[your CSS here]"> </p>`
ie. `<p style="color:red;">Please fill in the required fields.</p>`

After customizing the form, we need to create a page to put it on. So that it is clear, simply name the page **Contact Form** or something similar. To activate the contact form on this specific form, type in the following code: `%%wpcontactform%%`. This is a specific trigger set up by the plugin. Doing this adds the form to the page. It has a challenge question to prevent automated programs from sending you spam. It collects demographic information as well, so that you can properly respond. The information will be sent to the e-mail address you provided. The following screenshot shows the way the **Contact Form** will display on the pages:

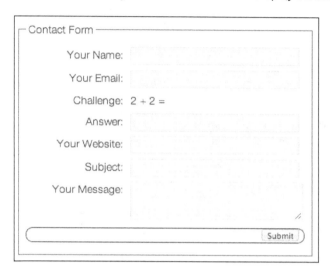

Blogging with students (Become an expert)

This recipe will look at different scenarios for blogging with students, and how to set those up with Edublogs.

Getting ready

There are at least two distinct ways to use blogging to help students. The first takes what you already do and just includes your class. Having a class blog, whether in addition to or as part of your current blog, is a simple and effective way to improve both community and communication in the classroom. A class blog is a blog that students, parents, and administrators can view to learn more about what is going on in your classroom.

Having a class blog gives parents a window into the world that their children spend so much time in. It opens up an avenue of communication between the teacher and the parents. It also helps to enable parents and guardians to better support their children. Posting your assignments, classwork, expectations, and so on gives the parents and guardians the tools that they need to help equip their children, whether it is simply by reinforcing the message that you are sending in class, or by knowing what to help them with and how. Including parents, and working with them, is one of the most powerful things we can do for our students.

Having a class blog can also help students extend the classroom beyond the physical walls and time constraints of school. The students can continue conversations about class topics in the comments of posts. They can stay updated and feel like a part of the class, even when they are not physically able to be in class. We want to give our students every opportunity possible to succeed; this is one opportunity that can be tremendously helpful for many students.

Class blogs also present the teacher with an opportunity and an obligation to teach about responsibility and digital citizenship. Students often do not realize the consequences of posting certain things online; publicly having discussions requires the teacher to set the students up with a solid foundation. While students will of course make mistakes, by educating them on how to act responsibly online, we can minimize the effects of any potential mistakes they may make.

Another way to include students in a class blog is to have students contribute posts. Depending on the age group, you can simply add the name of the student, or create accounts for them. Students can write what they have learned, take pictures of class work, or even post videos. It is often easier for the youngest students to articulate orally than through writing. If you do use a student's likeness, make sure you get written consent from the parents.

Pedagogically, I am always in favor of giving the kids choices. and enabling them to take control of their own learning. Having a class blog is an excellent tool; it is, though, limited in that students can usually only contribute in a limited manner through the comments. What if all of your students had their own blogs, their own spaces to write reflectively, to think academically, to explore their passions, and to discover their voices? Would this not be a powerful tool?

Think of the benefits that you get out of writing your own blog, if you have one, and reading the blogs of others, on topics in which you share an interest or passion. These benefits multiply manifold for students when they are equipped early on in their learning journey. Following are just a few of the positives that can come from students blogging:

- ▸ Develop habits of reflection and deep thought
- ▸ Learn to write responsibly by having a public audience
- ▸ Gain perspective by networking with people from around the world
- ▸ Increase passion by building a community of people with similar interests

▶ Deepen relationships with classmates by sharing and encouraging each other

▶ Find validation in realizing that other students are going through similar trials

▶ Build confidence by getting feedback from an authentic audience of both peers and adults

Having students start blogging today will not result in all of these things happening tomorrow; it is a time intensive process. It is more than worthwhile, but it is a process that will take a significant investment of time in teaching and training the students, as well as reading all of their blogs.

How to do it...

To create classes and student blogs, a Pro account is required. The way that student blogs work on Edublogs is that students create their own individual accounts on Edublogs and they are linked to a central teacher blog.

1. The first step is to create a class. On the navigation menu on the left, click on **My Class**, then **Create a Class**.

2. The next step, choosing the settings for the class, is vitally important. Let's look at each of the settings, and how they would practically impact a class. The class settings are showing in the following screenshot:

Settings	
Class Blog:	☐ This is a class blog
Allow students to post on the class blog:	○ Yes, no moderation - *able to publish posts on class blog*
	○ Yes, with moderation - *able to submit post pending review on class blog*
	⦿ No - *use if you want them to publish posts on their student blog*
Moderation on student blogs:	☐ I must approve all posts - *use if you want to check all posts before they are published*
	☐ I must approve all comments - *use if you want to check all comments before they are published*
Privacy:	⦿ Allow all visitors to all blogs
	○ Block search engines from all blogs, but allow normal visitors to see all blogs
	○ I would like only registered users of Edublogs.org to see each blog
	○ I would like only registered users of each blog to see it
	○ I would like anyone who provides the following password have access to all blogs
	Note: Anyone that is a registered user of this blog won't need this password.
	Password is the best privacy option if you only want other teachers, all students and family to view blogs
Teachers:	☐ bedelljason Edit user
Save	

3. The assumption here is that you are going to create a class where everyone has his or her own blog, as opposed to using this single blog as the place where each student writes. So, check the box that says **This is a class blog**. Following is a breakdown of some of the other important settings:

    a. **Allow students to post on the class blog**.

        Yes, no moderation: This allows students to write posts on the blog you are currently working on.

        No: This will force the student to write on their own blogs.

    b. **Moderation on student blogs**: This is optional, and you do not need to choose either option.

        I must approve all posts: No student posts will be published without your direct approval.

        I must approve all comments: This holds comments from publication until you check them for appropriateness. This can become difficult to do in a timely manner in larger classes, or classes that write often.

    c. **Privacy**: This relates to who is able to read the blog.

        Allow all visitors to all blogs: Anyone can view the blog.

        Block search engines from all blogs, but allow normal visitors to see all blogs: Search engines will not be able to see the students' posts, which will limit viewership. If your class has a specific audience in mind, it can be useful.

        I would like only registered users of Edublogs.org to see each blog: This limits the audience to only the users of Edublogs.

        I would like only registered users of each blog to see it: This limits the audience to only people who are members of the class.

        I would like anyone who provides the following password have access to all blogs: Severely limit access by only allowing those people who you have provided the password to.

    d. **Teachers**: Check yourself as the teacher.

You can go back to these settings at any time to make additional changes. For example, when I was a library media specialist last year, all of my third graders created blogs. While the students were first beginning, I limited the viewership to only those in the class. I did this so that I would have time to teach them what they needed to know about digital citizenship, online etiquette, editing, and appropriateness; it also gave the students a very safe place to experiment and make mistakes. Once the students were more skilled and comfortable with their blogging skills, I opened up the privacy settings and began to connect with other classes in different parts of the world.

How it works...

Once your settings are all chosen and submitted, the students need to create their accounts. It is tremendously helpful to have discussions beforehand with the students about expectations, standards, behavior, and exactly how blogging fits into your classroom.

When students create their accounts on Edublogs, the process is nearly identical to when teachers create accounts. The only difference is making sure they choose **Student** in the **blog type** field. Also, students do not have to provide an e-mail address, which is very useful, as most e-mail providers have Terms of Service that prevent young students from obtaining an account.

Once they have created their accounts, have the students log in. They need to go to the **My Class** section of the menu, and click on **Join a Class**. The students need to type in the first part of your blog URL. My example blog is `http://modellingbestpractice.edublogs.org`. So, students would type `modellingbestpractice` in the search field.

Once the students find the correct class, they need to click on the link **Send a request to join** to join the class. After this is done, you will see several new options in the **My Class** menu on your blog, as shown in the following screenshot:

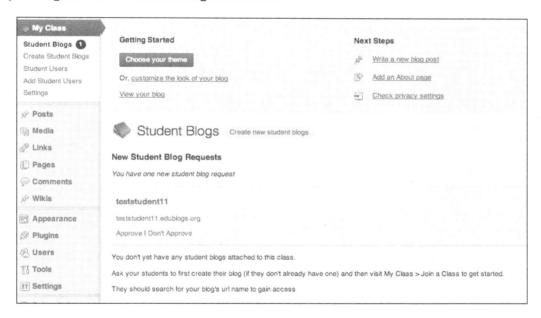

There will be a **Student Blogs** entry with a number representing the number of students waiting for approval into your class. Simply click on **Approve** on your students. Once all of the students do this, and you approve them, the blogs will all be linked, and operate according to the settings that you have chosen. Remember to consistently and constantly reinforce expectations and etiquette to students, especially early on in their blogging journeys. It will pay dividends throughout the year and beyond.

Analyzing statistics (Become an expert)

This recipe will show how to utilize statistics to better serve one's readers.

Getting ready

Statistics can be very useful in blogging. They do, however, require a Pro account on Edublogs. Statistics show how many visits your blog gets, which posts readers look at, and where they come from. There is a potential downside to looking at statistics, though. It is very easy to obsess over statistics. To combat this, remember why you started blogging and let that guide you. Statistics are a tool; they are not the only indicator of the success of a blog.

Developing a blog audience takes time. Even once your blog has a steady audience, there will be highs and lows. Following is a diagram of a random 30-day period from one of my blogs. There was one outstanding day, several good days, and some bad days. That is all fine; I know that I have a regular audience that will continue to come back, as we have developed a mutually beneficial relationship over several years based on quality content and authentic dialogue.

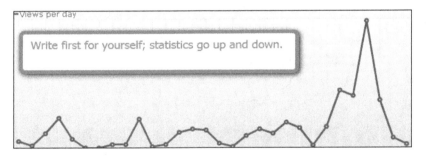

How to do it...

This recipe will show how to utilize statistics. The **Stats** section of the navigation menu has several different useful options, which are described in the following section:

1. The **Visitors Summary** page is the one most people look at most often. It is broken down into the following sections:

   ❑ **Last Visits**: This section shows a graph of the basic visits to the blog.

   ❑ **Visits Summary**: This section is a basic list of actions users have done, and how long they have visited the blog for.

❑ **Visitor World Map**: The map is an interactive display of where users have come from, shown in the following screenshot:

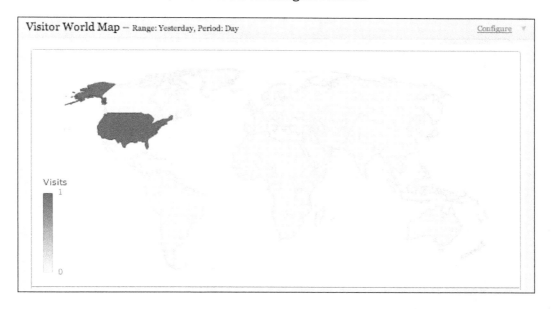

❑ **Visitors in Real Time**: This shows what pages users are looking at when you loaded the page.

❑ **Visitor Referrers**: This shows how users found the blog.

2. Each of these sections can be minimized by pressing the down arrow.

3. If you click and hold on the header, it can be moved and rearranged on the page.

4. Further, hovering over the headers displays a configure link. This gives you much more fine grained control over what the graphs show. For example, this lets you change the data period and the data analyzed by the **Last Visits** graph.

5. In addition, several of the graphs allow you to export them as an image or any of the following file types: CSV, Excel, JSON, PHP, and XML. Creative developers can do interesting things with that data.

How it works...

Following are the three other sections in the **Stats** that deal directly with important statistics.

1. **Content**: This page shows which pages readers looked at, and for how long.
2. **Referrers**: This page shows how users came to the blog, such as directly to the blog, from clicking on a search engine (as well as what was searched for), or clicking on a link from a website, such as Facebook or Twitter.
3. **Visitor Details**: This has demographic information about the readers, such as their screen resolution, what operating system they are using, or what browser they are using.

These statistics are a tool that collectively can tell you a lot about your readers. Looking at your statistics, there are many questions that you can ask yourself.

▶ Are there any topical trends in terms of what posts users visit most or spend the most time reading?

▶ How are users finding your blog (search engine, a particular social network, and so on)?

▶ Are your visitors from a specific locale?

▶ Are most of your readers using mobile devices or traditional desktops/laptops (mobile lends itself to shorter posts)?

These are just a few of many examples. Statistics should never be the only impetus when determining what and how to write, but they do show what your readers are looking for. If part of the reason for blogging is to make a difference, it is helpful to know what readers' needs are, and to try to fill those needs.

There's more...

There is one more option in the **Stats** menu for advanced users. If you feel that you need even more detailed statistics, Edublogs supports **Google Analytics**. Analytics is a system built by Google for tracking website visitors. Sign up for a Google Analytics account at `http://www.google.com/analytics/`. Then, go to the **Stats** menu, click on the **Google Analytics** entry, and add you Google Analytics tracking code.

About Packt Publishing

Packt, pronounced 'packed', published its first book "*Mastering phpMyAdmin for Effective MySQL Management*" in April 2004 and subsequently continued to specialize in publishing highly focused books on specific technologies and solutions.

Our books and publications share the experiences of your fellow IT professionals in adapting and customizing today's systems, applications, and frameworks. Our solution based books give you the knowledge and power to customize the software and technologies you're using to get the job done. Packt books are more specific and less general than the IT books you have seen in the past. Our unique business model allows us to bring you more focused information, giving you more of what you need to know, and less of what you don't.

Packt is a modern, yet unique publishing company, which focuses on producing quality, cutting-edge books for communities of developers, administrators, and newbies alike. For more information, please visit our website: www.packtpub.com.

Writing for Packt

We welcome all inquiries from people who are interested in authoring. Book proposals should be sent to author@packtpub.com. If your book idea is still at an early stage and you would like to discuss it first before writing a formal book proposal, contact us; one of our commissioning editors will get in touch with you.

We're not just looking for published authors; if you have strong technical skills but no writing experience, our experienced editors can help you develop a writing career, or simply get some additional reward for your expertise.

WordPress 3.5 Complete: Third Edition

ISBN: 978-1-78216-240-7   Paperback: 446 pages

Make your first end-to-end website from scratch with WordPress

1. Learn how to build a WordPress site quickly and effectively

2. Find out how to create content that's optimized to be published on the Web

3. Learn the basics of working with WordPress themes and playing with widgets

Drupal 7 Social Networking

ISBN: 978-1-84951-600-6   Paperback: 328 pages

Build a social or community website with friend lists, groups, custom user profiles, and much more

1. Step-by-step instructions for putting together a social networking site with Drupal 7

2. Customize your Drupal installation with modules and themes to match the needs of almost any social networking site

3. Allow users to collaborate and interact with each other on your site

Please check **www.PacktPub.com** for information on our titles

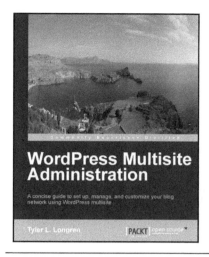

www.ingramcontent.com/pod-product-compliance
Lightning Source LLC
LaVergne TN
LVHW080105070326
832902LV00014B/2431

* 9 7 8 1 8 4 9 6 9 8 6 2 7 *